# Misfortune Cookies

SIDNEY S. PRASAD

ISBN: 1927676290
ISBN-13:978-1-927676-29-5

# DEDICATION

I dedicate this book to anyone who will read it and leave
me an awesome review!

# CONTENTS

## ACKNOWLEDGMENTS

Can you imagine if restaurants actually printed how they felt on a fortune cookie inscription?

# 1 SERIOUSLY?

The health inspector doesn't know this restaurant exists.

The guy sitting next to you is a serial killer.

Now you know what dogs taste like!

The cook didn't wash his hands after using the shitter!

We are environmentally friendly at this restaurant and recycle food.

I warmed your rolls in my underwear.

Why do you think they call it pea soup?

Please don't sue us!

Leave a big tip please because I need to buy a rat trap.

Go home so the mice and cockroaches can get some sleep in here.

Were you drunk when met your wife?

You should lend your razor to your hairy wife.

.

My boss lets his mafia buddies cremate bodies in the oven.

Did your husband make you order from the children's menu again?

Can I go skiing on your nose?

## 2 WRONG COOKIE

It's hard to cut a onion when your ass is itchy.

Did you take a second mortgage out to tip me that two dollars?

If you are reading this you are the biggest fucken idiot!

Don't look now there's a pubic hair in your egg roll.

# Your kid is exceptional my ass!

Your noodles were boiled in toilet water.

Do you know what the word "DIET" means?

Your husband is having an affair.

Quit fucken smiling!

Pull up your pants because you got more crack than Harlem!

There are love stains on your chair!

# You farted didn't you?

I recognize your date from America's Most Wanted.

Over a thousand people used your plate and utensils!

Are you looking for some company tonight?  Because my grandpa is really horny!

You're pretty intelligent because you just spent $30 on a $9 dollar bottle of wine.

I was having a pick and flick adventure while preparing your chow mein.

Can I have your wife for dessert?

You pervert!

Does your welfare officer know that you are splurging on this $5.99 buffet?

Get the fuck out of here!

I hope you didn't eat the lunch special today!

Do you really think you're lucky?

# The health inspector takes bribes!

The cook lost his bandage.

There is a hidden camera in the shitter.

I gave myself a pedicure with your butter knife.

When was the last time you took a shower?

We used dog shit to fertilize our vegetable garden in the back.

You got spinach in your teeth.

# Do you model for secondhand store flyers?

I'm going to tell your date that you used a coupon you cheat shit!

SIDNEY S. PRASAD

Eat shit and die!

That green tea on your table is made from fresh mule piss.

You are the world's biggest asshole!

I had sex with your wife!

Now you know what cats taste like!

This restaurant was built over a pet cemetery.

Google the word, "shit" to find out what our secret ingredient is.

Did you and your wife actually produce those hideous kids?

Do you see that exit sign?

Hey lardass you broke my chair.

Thanks for the shitty tip maybe you should audition for Extreme Cheapskates!

Have you ever heard of
deodorant?

Wipe that shit smear smile off your face!

## 5 HA HA!

Our chef is illiterate and therefore doesn't check the expiry dates.

Your face looks like pepperoni pizza without the toppings.

Why don't you chew with your mouth closed for a change?

Shh listen to the cockroaches underneath your table.

Flush the toilet next time you jack ass!

Your daughter's a little whore!

This restaurant used to be a sexually transmitted disease clinic.

Hey shithead you are what you eat!

Children are starving and you just ate enough food to feed an entire village.

The chef is doing community service here because he used to run a daycare.

The local sperm bank gave us a deal on the secret sauce!

I saw your grandma at the nudie bar.

The chef used your chopsticks to clean his ears.

The kitchen ran out of hand
soap two months ago!

# Thank you don't come again!

# 6 COME AGAIN?

I had sex with the cleaning lady on your table last night.

I left a present for you in the shitter.

I hope you have good health insurance.

Hey kid, there is no Santa Claus and the Easter Bunny is dead!

I thought you were an animal right activist? Oh well I guess you couldn't resist the taste of rat meat!

Do you want to buy a used condom?

Your kids are brats!

Thanks for leaving a used tampon in the washroom sink!

Our dishwasher hasn't shown up to work in a week and my dog licks the plates clean.

I think your girlfriend wants to fuck me!

Your mama has pierced nipples!

Did you notice that the plum sauce was extra sweet today?

Please ignore the nose hair in your Buddha's Feast.

There is a prostitution ring operated from this restaurant.

Do you always use a debit card when paying for a $5 meal?

When was the last time you changed your underwear?

I wish we had a drive-thru so I wouldn't have to stare at that hideous mole on your face!

# Hands above the table!

Quit ordering the cheapest booze on the menu and go to your rehab session!

Is that your probation officer that you're dining with?

# What's that creature climbing up your leg?

You got an ugly family!

Free refills doesn't mean to bring a jerrican and fill it with pop!

Are you too busy to say grace before you chow?

Do you want a takeout bag for your food or to cover your date's face?

It's amazing how wonton soup broth can soften up old toe nail clippings!

Your date just paid for the entire meal with change.

Nice suit did you buy it from a garage sale?

Don't you love it when someone brings a crying baby to their Valentine's Day dinner?

Don't open the door next to the washroom!

# 8 FOOL

Who is the retro barber that cut your hair?

There is meat in the vegetarian dishes.

Thank you for helping us solve the city's rat problem by ordering the special!

I shoved your chopsticks up my ass before I set it on your table!

# Lose some weight!

You're a bastard child!

I bet shit taste better than your meal!

We have been using the same oil since Bush was in office.

# Your girlfriend is loose!

# Get the fuck out I want to close now!

The owner's child was delivered on your table.

You just used recycled toilet paper.

My dentures were soaking in your jug of water!

I know you didn't wash your hands in the shitter because I didn't hear the water running.

I love your "my shit don't stink" smile.

## 9 VERY SAD

Thanks for that food stamp tip!

Thank you for being the chef's guinea pig!

Hey fucker you're not allowed to smuggle in your own soft drinks in the restaurant!

Get your hand out of your pants!

Halloween is over you should take off your mask!

Your credit declined ha ha deadbeat!

Was your wife a mail-order bride?

Get out or I will call
immigration on your ass!

# Is this your first time using utensils?

What street corner did you rent
your date from?

There was lice attached to that hair in your soup.

Thanks for the lousy tip you cheap shit!

You just ate a meal cooked at a restaurant that promotes child labor.

All the frying pans were dirty so
I used my grandma's bed pan to
fry the dumplings.

Your daddy's having an affair
with your teacher.

# 10 WHY?

A cult leader owns this restaurant.

Did you buy your cologne from a camping store? Because you smell like mosquito repellent!

# Buy some dental floss please!

You got a stain on your sweater.

You should have left your shitty kids with the babysitter!

Did you escape from a mental institution?

The only reason why you were born was because your mama forgot to take her pill!

Quit playing pocket pool,
because the referee is a dick!

# Did you enjoy the maggots?

You have hairy palms.

You're sitting in the wrong section; you should be dining in the mutant area of the restaurant with the rest of your clan.

Clothing is optional in the kitchen and all the cooks are sweaty and hairy.

You just ate toxic waste!

If you don't leave I'm going to break your bones and make a wish.

# ABOUT THE AUTHOR

Sidney S. Prasad is an author on a quest to make the world laugh. His work is focused on entertaining people with his dry-humored novels. Sidney S. Prasad personally believes laughter is the best cure for all of life's ups and downs.

**Some other humorous books written by Sidney S. Prasad include:**

*How To Piss Off A Telemarketer,*
*My Bipolar Manager,*
*Don't Ask Dumb Questions!,*
*My Stupid CEO,*
*Plenty Of Freaks: Are You Sold On Online Dating?*
*Plenty Of Freaks: Worst Online Dating Mistakes*
**and**
*Corny Names & Stupid Places*

www.ingramcontent.com/pod-product-compliance
Lightning Source LLC
Chambersburg PA
CBHW060832050426
42453CB00008B/656

* 9 7 8 1 9 2 7 6 7 6 2 9 5 *